THE TREE WHISPERER

A collection of stories told to me by TREES.

MICHELLE BEAUREGARD

Copyright@2022 by Michelle Beauregard

All rights reserved. No parts of this publication may be reproduced, stored in a retrieval system, or transmitted, in any form or by any means, electronic, mechanical, photocopying, recording or otherwise, without the written prior permission of the publisher.

ISBN: 978-0-9699931-6-2

Edited by: Karen Breakey

Front cover photo: Martin Dahinden

Photographer: Martin Dahinden

Author biography photo: Babar Javed

Book design and layout: Daiana Morales

Icons made by Freepik from www.rawpixel.com

Acknowledgment

This book is a team effort, so I would sincerely like to thank my husband and photographer, Martin Dahinden, for fearlessly venturing on the road, believing in magic, and meeting each tree with much love and gratitude. Reiki is the foundation of these writings, and without it, I believe I never would have been able to embark on this book. I offer my profound gratitude to my Reiki teacher and mother-in-law, Wanja Twan, who opened the door to the wisdom of trees through Reiki.

I would also like to thank my dear friend, Karen Breakey, who embraced the job of editing with much patience, gusto, and enthusiasm always. Much gratitude to my sister-in-law, Anneli Twan, for her heartfelt support and encouragement on all levels with this book. Finally, a big thank you to my friend, Paul Jerry, for his editorial insights and wisdom.

Dedication

This book is dedicated to my husband, Martin,
and to the trees of the world.

Introduction

A JOURNEY ROOTED IN CONNECTION

The messages from trees started to form this book back in 2018, on a visit to Hong Kong. Amidst the bustling city, with its mix of urban energy and serene natural spaces, I encountered an ancient Banyan tree, its roots woven into the fabric of the massive stone walls it grew upon. I couldn't resist placing my hands on its gnarled bark, allowing Reiki energy to flow between us.

In that moment, something extraordinary happened—a dialogue of energy and imagery began. Words flowed into my mind, and I had the presence of mind to write them down. It was an auspicious beginning, an invitation from the natural world to listen, observe, and remember a long-lost awareness and connection.

THE LANGUAGE OF TREES

Over time, I learned that trees have their own way of communicating. Sometimes, they would introduce themselves by name. Other times, they offered fragments—poems, historical tales, or vivid imagery. Some messages came as gentle whispers, others as clear directives.

I recorded these encounters faithfully. I chose not to research the geography or history of the locations where these trees grew. This book is not a scientific study but rather a stream of consciousness, guided by Reiki and intuition, capturing the pure essence of each exchange.

MY REIKI JOURNEY

Reiki, in the lineage I follow, is a practical energy science—simple, profound, and accessible to anyone willing to learn from a Reiki Master. Reiki originated from Japan in the early 1900s, and the word Reiki means Universal life energy. It is a system of great simplicity since only the hands are required. This energy flows out through the practitioner's hands, helping restore balance and harmony on the physical, mental, and emotional levels. It can be used on humans as well as animals and plant life.

Reiki can also open channels of intuitive insight for the practitioner and the recipient. In my experience, the more I incorporate Reiki into my daily life, the more intuitive information becomes available. There is a deepening sense of trust in Reiki as one learns to listen to their hands during sessions.

Over time, Reiki has become a sixth sense for me. It is much different than the physical sense of touch, creating a gentle yet powerful connection.

Today, there are as many Reiki lineages as there are rivers flowing into the ocean—each with its own best practices, shaped by the teacher and their unique lineage.

In this book, my intention is to share the way I learned Reiki—to inspire others to trust their intuitive connection with the natural world and to experience Reiki as a living, breathing presence in their daily lives.

A FORTUNATE MEETING WITH MY TEACHER, WANJA TWAN

I was fortunate to learn Reiki from my wonderful mother-in-law, Wanja Twan, in 1994. Wanja was one of Mrs. Hawayo Takata's original students in Canada. Mrs. Takata learned Reiki in Japan, and as a Reiki Master, taught Reiki extensively during her lifetime. Mrs. Takata brought Reiki to Canada in the 1970s where she taught many classes in rural British Columbia. Wanja met her most respected teacher, Mrs. Takata, in 1978 in Lumby, B.C. She went on to become a Reiki Master in 1979 and one of the original 22 Reiki Masters in North America that Mrs. Takata trained during her lifetime. Mrs. Takata passed away in 1980.

My connection with Wanja began long before I became her Reiki student. In 1972, when I was just eight years old, my mother enrolled me in a weaving course at Wanja's farm and traditional weaving school in Cherryville B.C. She taught me to weave on a wooden loom. Though our paths diverged after that summer, fate brought us together again 20 years later when I married her son in 1994.

Learning Reiki from Wanja in 1994 felt like stepping out of a dark room into brilliant light. Reiki became that light for me. I became a Reiki Master in 1997 and was blessed to study with

Wanja until her passing in 2019, growing not only as her student but as her family.

THE SIMPLICITY OF REIKI IN THIS LINEAGE

In this lineage, Reiki is wonderfully simple. All you need are your hands and your intention.

- <u>First Degree Reiki:</u> Where one learns a hands-on technique for self-care and to treat family, friends, and neighbours.
- <u>Second Degree Reiki:</u> The practice expands to distance healing, enabling practitioners to send Reiki across time and space.
- <u>Reiki Mastery:</u> The practitioner learns to teach and pass on this healing art to others.

This system worked with excellent results for my dear teacher, Wanja Twan, for 40 years, for Mrs. Takata for over 40 years, and for me since I learned in 1994. Its strength lies in its simplicity, creating an intuitive connection to the flow of life and all living things.

REIKI AS AN INTUITIVE CONNECTION TO NATURE

One of the most extraordinary aspects of Reiki is how it bridges our connection to the natural world. When I place my hands on a tree, I don't just feel its bark or its stillness—I receive information.

It's as if the tree and I are speaking in a language beyond words.

All matter is made of energy. Reiki simply allows us to tap into this universal energy with focused intention, reminding us that we are never separate from nature, each other, or the life force that flows through everything.

A UNIVERSAL PRACTICE FOR EVERYDAY LIFE

Reiki is universally accessible regardless of one's beliefs or background. It fits into daily life, offering support for physical emotional, and mental health.

My life's passion is to teach Reiki and share the practical, hands-on wisdom passed down to me by Wanja Twan. Whether in person, through workshops, or in moments of quiet reflection with a student, I remain devoted to this practice because I've seen how it can transform lives—just as it transformed mine.

Although I grew up on a farm in B.C. and always felt connected to animals and nature, learning Reiki profoundly transformed my relationship to energy and healing. When I received my First-Degree Reiki training in 1994, I had been living with chronic kidney pain for a decade. Western medicine dealt with the symptoms but could not find the root cause of the imbalance. A few months after learning Reiki, the kidney pain was completely gone—and that was 30 years ago.

LESSONS FROM MY TEACHER, WANJA TWAN

Wanja was my first teacher in connecting with trees and nature through Reiki.

Wanja often spoke of how trees have memory and how they can even recognize individuals over time.

"When we drive on the same roads over the remote B.C. mountain passes year after year, the trees on either side of the road can sense our presence and even recognize us."

Wanja listened to the forest as though she was the forest itself. She taught me about the concept of the Mother Tree, a central figure holding energy for the forest, facilitating a silent exchange of wisdom and life force.

When we cleared land to build a cabin in the early 1990s, Wanja identified the main trees and rocks holding the land's energy. With Reiki, she gently relieved the stress caused by the disruption, bringing balance back to the area. Every rock, tree, mountain, and stream held a story, and through Reiki, Wanja brought these hidden narratives to light.

Wanja had a profound ability to be still and listen. In her stillness, she accessed a peaceful clarity and an expanded view of life. Her physical presence seemed to illuminate answers to unspoken questions effortlessly and without force.

GUIDED BY REIKI AND NATURE

Since first learning Reiki, I have felt guided—almost as if an unseen hand directs me to the right trees at the right time. It's as though the boundaries between my hands and the trees dissolve, leaving only connection.

The trees I wrote about are scattered across urban centers in Canada, Mexico, Sweden, Britain, China, Vietnam, France, Switzerland, and Spain. These locations were not pre-planned; they simply appeared along my journey like hidden teachers waiting to be found.

The trees responded not to my voice or questions, but to my presence. It felt like meeting old friends, standing together in a space of quiet recognition and shared energy.

A CHRONOLOGICAL EXPLORATION

The stories in this book are presented chronologically, unfolding as they happened. With each tree, I felt an increasing awareness that the fate of humanity and trees is inseparable.

We are not separate from nature. What we do to nature, we do to ourselves.

THE TEACHINGS OF REIKI AND INTUITION

For over 25 years, Reiki has taught me that energy flows wherever intention goes—whether directed towards a person, animal, plant, or situation. Reiki doesn't require force or control—it requires presence and trust.

One of Wanja's favorite exercises to demonstrate our connection with nature was to erase small clouds from the sky with focused intention. She encouraged everybody to try this fun activity. It's such a simple act, yet profoundly symbolic of our capacity to co-create with nature.

AN OFFERING OF GRATITUDE

This book is an offering—a reflection of the joy, wonder, and wisdom I've received from the tree world.

It is my belief that to be human is to live in relationship—with the water, sky, earth, and all life forms sharing this planet.

We are not superior to our environment; we are woven into it, as inseparable as roots are from soil.

I hope these stories ignite a sense of delight, curiosity, and reverence for the world of trees. May they serve as an invitation to explore your own connection with nature and Reiki.

With gratitude,
Michelle Beauregard

Table of Contents

Hong Kong 2018 .... p.2

Vietnam 2018 .... p.12

United Kingdom 2018 .... p.21

Sweden 2018.. p.23

Canada 2018.. p.27

Mexico 2019 .... p.45

United Kingdom 2020 .... p.66

France 2020 .... p.80

Switzerland 2020... p.95

Spain 2020 .... p.99

Sweden 2020... p.110

Canada 2022... p.114

Call to Action... p.117

Author's Biography... p.118

2018

Tree in Kennedy Town wall, Hong Kong, China 2018

The Tree Whisperer

After spending the day exploring the streets of Hong Kong, I found myself drawn to a shady green bank of large Banyan trees. Their gnarled and twisted roots reached with exposed outstretched tendrils down and into the rocky cliff. The air around the trees was like a little oasis of oxygen in the smog-filled city. A small green bench at the base of the roots was a perfect invitation to take a well-needed pause to rejuvenate my tired feet.

Whenever I am in a new city, I make it a point to thank the "nature beings" of the area for inviting me. On this day, a huge Banyan tree captured my attention. I carefully placed my hands on the roots that were covering the rocks, silently introduced myself, and gave thanks for the opportunity. When I place my hands on a living thing with good intention, Reiki goes there. At this time, the tree felt very tired and old. I continued with my hands-on approach and asked the tree if it had any messages for me.

In my mind, I heard a silent voice thanking me for taking the time to give a greeting.

When I place my hands on living trees, I am open to receive information by listening to my hands. Although the tree is not actually "speaking," there is a dialogue that happens, and communication is felt on a level without words.

For best results, place your hands on the trunk of a tree and make your intentions known to the tree. This can be done in a silent, thoughtful way or by speaking the words. I explain that the information is going to be used for educational purposes to the benefit of all living beings.

This old tree seemed to have an enthusiastic response to my hands. The first feeling I had was that the tree was so grateful for this contact.

TREE: *We are so happy that you have stopped by. We are one and the same as you on Mother Earth and are always open to contact of a positive nature. In fact, we would ask that each human take the time to slow down and feel our Oneness each day as it helps heal the whole living, breathing Earth that we all call home. If you humans slowed down, then you would sense that we are truly part of your consciousness. It is not easy, but we are patient. We are tired of the pollution and disrespect. We suffer from disease just like humans. But we can help each other.*

Take time to be around trees and understand that we can help recharge your energy levels. You can give us your negative feelings just by sitting next to us or putting your arms around us. We can take your hardships and sink them deep into the earth to disperse them and send up nourishment in the form of grounding and connection. That is how interconnectedness works; we help look after one another.

The tree was just getting started…

TREE: *We would like to invite all humans to plant trees whenever possible. We can usually regenerate ourselves naturally, but all the environmental changes and industrial growth are making that increasingly difficult.*

So, to put it bluntly… without trees, humans will not be able to survive. You need us for oxygen. We need humanity to reach out in this way and make contact by planting trees in cities, schools, homes, and farms. This helps ensure the survival of us mother, Gaia, and all life.

We benefit from the energy exchange with humans as there is love and gratitude that is released from the heart when humans are surrounded by nature, and this adds to a higher vibration for all consciousness. There is no division between human, plant, and animal. We are all part of the same energy field and are an important part of the whole in all forms.

Of course, sitting in the cool, oxygen-rich environment under the tree, I was already noticing how my lungs felt better after the smog and traffic-filled day. A certain peacefulness washed over me and calmed my over-stimulated brain.

The stream of information continued to come from the tree.

TREE: *Water is also an issue. In the cities, we must cope with much concrete, and this slows our access to natural water supplies. Clean water is also a life force upon which we are all dependent. In some places, we need special care until our roots reach deep enough. That is why we need the help of all humans, especially in cities; they must be our voice, so to speak.*

Humans think that we can't talk, but we have always been communicating. Some hear our messages more clearly than others. We are just on a different, slower time frame than you. From our perspective, one of your 12-hour days is like the time it takes for a butterfly to flutter its wings. So, you see, we notice and communicate with all of life but not in the same way as you. Don't think we aren't trying to get through to you... some people are just so preoccupied with the daily rush of business and life that they are not able to tune into the subtle and slow rhythm of the inner world. This is a place guided by intuition and the seasons. We can communicate with other plants, animals, and trees a great distance away from here in our own unique way.

I feel the tension drain out of my arms from the day's activities, and my breathing slows to a regular pace as my hands are still on the tree roots. This tree has given me a real boost in exchange for taking the time to listen. My new role as the messenger for the trees and one I feel is sacred. This is an exchange for the life-affirming energy from my host, the magnificent Banyan tree in the streets of Hong Kong.

Tree in Intersection, Hong Kong, China 2018

Being open to receiving an invitation to communicate with a tree is an exercise in trust. Being present in the moment helps me open a heartfelt dialogue on the nonverbal level with surprising results.

This Banyan tree stands in the middle of a busy intersection in an action-packed shopping district in Hong Kong.

A huge digital billboard flashes along one side of the square, where the branches hang protectively. The rush of passing traffic ensures a constant buzz, punctuated by honking horns and the loud clacking of streetcar wheels. A seemingly unusual place to find a 100-year-old Banyan tree, but the location was once serene. Walking up to the tree, I put my hands on its trunk, feeling the life force of this living being pulsing like a flowing river, beckoning me. Thus invited, I introduce myself.

The formalities over, I ask the tree if it has any messages for humanity. The first response tells me this tree has been wanting to contact a human who was listening for a long time.

TREE: *I sit on the edge of this intensely busy crosswalk; hundreds of people stream past me each day, oblivious to my presence. My aerial roots stretch and dangle, contacting commuters as they pass. Like delicate fingers, my roots stroke the top of their heads as they walk. I sense their thoughts and ideas and help them connect to the realm of nature I embody. In the past 50 years, nature has been forced to make way for the growth of the city, but we trees can't keep up with the rapid pace of change.*

These high buildings block the natural sunlight from reaching my leaves: I miss the warmth. At the same time, I send out branches to try to shield myself from the intense, cold, dead light from the massive, unrelenting video billboard. A poor substitute for the sun, it offers no warmth or light for growth.

We trees are strong and work to adapt to any situation, but under these lifeless conditions, we struggle. Only 50 years ago, this place was green and alive, and we were all connected. We would love to connect again to the living, to the people and birds and wildlife and the life-giving sun, as in earlier times.

An old Buddhist priest once came here daily to say his morning prayers and meet locals to talk about life and nature. Such good thoughts and deeds remain with us trees always. We record and recognize people and their vibrations around us with an intricate web of invisible fields. The arrangement is beneficial. The good thoughts and ideas I've absorbed can be distributed back to all living beings who are aware of my presence.

My message to people is to make the time to slow down and connect to all the natural world around them. Their minds and hearts will feel better, and so will we trees.

Tree in Kennedy Town trail, Hong Kong, China 2018

This old Banyan tree is located on a street in Kennedy Town, Hong Kong. It's part of a retaining wall that protects the steep mountain slopes from collapsing into the road. This group of trees is very famous around Hong Kong, with its root system exposed to a busy thoroughfare.

I place my hands on one of the tree roots and introduce myself, taking a moment of stillness to know and listen deeply.

The tree responds with a flow of information.

TREE: *We trees have been here for about 100 years. When this wall was built, we grew out of the rock at the top and found the growing situation to be very well suited to our needs. This steep vertical wall provides us with ample space in which to send our aerial roots down to the ground. This is how we can maximise water, light, and nourishment for our whole system. We consider ourselves to be a part of this retaining wall and part of our role here is as community members.*

Although we don't speak your language, we do communicate with people in the neighbourhood here. Every time someone walks past us; we pick up their thought forms and record them. We send the energy either up to the leaves in our canopy to be released or down into our roots to be grounded. We trees are part of the history in this area and recognize that humans and trees are all community members.

Tree at gate, Marble Mountains, Danang, Vietnam 2018

This tree sits among a series of ancient mountain caves, hidden temples, and winding steep trails among giant carved Buddhas and dragons.

TREE: *I am the messenger between this world and the planets. These mountains are built on energy lines that unite the earth realm with the realm of the skies. We trees are the messengers between the lower and upper worlds. We record information about human activity in these five-element mountains: metal, water, wood, fire, and earth.*

Tree at cave, Marble Mountains, Danang, Vietnam 2018

TREE: *Water dragons within the ground here protect the Marble Mountains. Water flows to all of us trees here, carrying subtle vibrations of information. Each mountain is a vortex linked to a network of water energy lines. Western culture understands dragons to be in the physical form, but they also exist in the ethereal realm, invisible to the eye. The dragons travel along these lines and connect energy to many places. Dragons are a powerful archetype in Vietnam and a sacred part of the history of this land.*

The Marble Mountains are very energising for all who come here. Many temples and pilgrimage routes nestle amongst the winding mountain paths.

Tree at Forbidden Purple City and Citadel, Hue, Vietnam 2018

TREE: *I have been here for over 50 years. I was planted in the earth during the reign of one of the last emperors of Vietnam.*

Here, in the Forbidden Purple City, the emperor is the son of heaven and the head of the dragon, so many special ceremonies protected this lineage. All the previous emperors had special geomancers who held ceremonies to protect and energise this land for the people. The emperor was seen as the dragon head and all my roots tap into this old earth magic. Geomancers and wise Elders, Feng Shui masters, and mandarins chose this land to build the Forbidden Purple City. That is why the Citadel is built on the northern bank of the Perfume River in Hue.

This magic is still on the earth. The protection ceremonies were so powerful, but now these old ways are mostly forgotten. A new time has come with more freedom and influences from the outside world. This is part of a big global shift in the consciousness of humanity.

I am one of the last remaining old wise trees of the Forbidden Purple City and one of the last of my kind. Thank you for taking the time to listen to my story. I saw you walking through the field and recognized you to be an open channel for communication between us trees and humans. We connected through our mutual interest in inter-species dialogue. The water dragons are still here but lie dormant under the earth. There will come a time in the future when they awaken to help humanity. Their energy is shared through the collective memory of us trees to visitors of the Forbidden Purple City. Some people sense this energy while others do not. Many Vietnamese people make offerings at their homes and workplaces in the form of treats, sweets, flowers, or incense to their ancestors. The Vietnamese connection to spiritual realms can also include recognizing the spirit of the tree in its roots, leaves, and branches. My history is not separate from this human story. The old trees like me must be kept alive and preserved to protect these locations and our stories for future generations.

Tree at Hoi An intersection, Vietnam 2018

TREE: *I have been here a very long time. I have been so successful because I sit on the banks of the Thu Bon River. The river is a symbol of success for this community. Since the beginning of civilization, humans have been in this area. The river provides wealth for all.*

I have watched goods and services being transported here from all over the world regardless of borders. No borders withstand the test of time; they have changed many times due to politics and economy over the centuries. But the river remains—the common thread linking abundance to business and trade right here. My roots go deep into the river and feel the strength that the water current gives to the people. This energy attracts people who, in turn, sustain the interactions.

One message I have for people is that I feel the water is suffering due to pollution caused by humans. The river is filled with garbage and this, in turn, affects the land, including the trees. And I am not one tree but many, as my roots connect me to a community. What we do to one part of this system is what we do to ourselves.

Tree in Soho District, London, UK 2018

TREE: *My name is Theodore Poet-Tree.*

The art of the tree lies beneath the snow-covered ground... a still life portrait covered in dirt, worms, and moss.

The seasons change to spring and the thaw awakens one's heart.

I am that portrait of an old man's wisdom etched in the lines of a craggy face worn in the ancient crusty exterior.

Beneath the bark, my bite is a patient whisper in the murmuring of the leaves. What's that? Speak up, I can't hear you.

My voice lies. Somewhere deep in the earth and with each step of your foot upon the pallet of colours of green, brown, and black beneath your sole, you can feel my heartbeat, a deep tremor in the core of your being. I am old but will never forget you. Your thoughts are new growth pouring into my outstretched branches pulling tendrils of light from the sun.

As my hands lay upon the tree, I heard a few tradespeople talking as they walked past:

"What's that woman doing to the tree?"

"Well, don't you know? Of course, she's giving that tree some energy."

Tree at Adolf Frederiks Church, Stockholm, Sweden 2018

TREE: *My name is Whispering-in-the-Ear.*

Prayers made here by humans take hold in the soil and they nourish the ground. We trees pull up their energy in our roots and send them out through our leaves and branches to benefit all who pass by.

This church is built on earth that was on a pilgrimage route—a mysterious portal that was important to ancient Vikings.

Each of us trees surrounding this sanctuary have special tree spirit beings that live with us. They protect the area, and they protect us. Many tree spirits gather in this area as they come from all over the country.

Note: This is the church where former Swedish Prime Minister Olaf Palme was buried in 1986.

Tree on street in Stockholm, Sweden, 2018

Michelle Beauregard

TREE: *Thoughts of the old ones in the branches and leaves...*

Whispering wind circulates those thoughts to everyone in the neighbourhood, anchoring and connecting all the thoughts to make a community of people and trees.

Tree in Sidney, BC, Canada 2018

TREE: *I was home to thousands of insects and birds.*

Now I lie on the ground, roots cut off but still connected to my essence.

My roots recall the motion of tiny wings and the soft tickle of ants. Now, the bird nest has fallen with dismayed bird parents looking on.

My destiny: to return to the earth.

This is a photo of me with my Reiki Master and mother-in-law, Wanja Twan. It seems fitting that we were both there to see a fallen tree together as Wanja was the head of our family tree and the head of my Reiki lineage. She was the most marvellous root teacher for my spiritual journey and constant source of inspiration for my Reiki practise.

Tree in Bastion Square, Victoria, BC, Canada 2018

TREE: *I bear witness to the ones who were hanged by the neck. This is an area where there were public hangings. Many of the men who died were buried right in the ground where they were hung. The spirits are very close.*

Tree in English Bay, Vancouver, BC, Canada 2018

TREE: *My nickname is Juicy Fruit. My purpose is to extend an invitation to all life forms to come and visit, but the bright red of my berries is a message to all not to eat my fruit. However, in my energy field, I attract many winged ones—birds and insects alike. The birds love my dense foliage, and they scratch and peck at the ground all around my trunk for bugs. In this way, I get more fertiliser... and they get a nice, tasty snack. We help each other out.*

The woodpeckers come and peck on my trunk to find insects as well. As you can see, I am covered with their tattoos. I really don't mind, though, as this also helps fertilize the area where my roots grow deep into the earth.

My message to humans is to look around and support those who are in your immediate circle, for, in this generous act, you will be assisted in the form of gratitude, and this will nourish your being. You don't have to look very far as these people will come to you. Humans supporting one another helps the web of life and Mother Earth's immunity system. All connected. Tapped in, so to speak.

How's that for some juicy news? Thank you for stopping by today. You are loved.

English Bay, Vancouver, BC, Canada 2018

TREES: *We are a group collective called the Bamboo Zone. When the wind blows, our trunks rub together, causing friction and tension. But we share root systems and, in this way, receive nourishment and protection, so we are completely dependent on one another. We are a collective for our survival. If we were just one bamboo, we would not last long. We require many shoots to provide enough roots and strength. Our leaves are on the top of everyone, but all the energy is exchanged among us in the root system.*

Although we are everyone, we are also a group. Without community, we could not exist. We share resources even though being this close together can cause stress and strain from our trunks rubbing against each other. Sometimes we break branches but, still, we remain stronger.

We are 50 years old, and we were planted by a bird. The river here is also part of our community and helps us get food and water each day.

Food also comes in the way of dead fish from the river, nourishing the soil.

Our message to humans is to slow down and realise your connection to all species on this planet. Whenever we bamboo get in conflict with people, we must, when the time is right, grow from what we experience and keep striving towards the light. Humans once had an ability to tune into other life forms and one day this natural inclination will return, helping restore balance.

Tree in Nitobe Gardens, Vancouver, BC, Canada 2018

TREE: *Learning is a road we all venture upon. I was planted as one of the first trees here by a man who helped create this garden. He passed away many years ago, but he is remembered as the new generations of gardeners keep working here.*

I grow out into the path to reach out and contact all those who pass by. The gentle spirit of the man who created this garden is remembered when people spend time here receiving feelings of love and caring for nature.

The rock path in front of me represents life's journey and how each one of us walks a path created by those who came before... each at our own pace, in our own time. We cannot be in a hurry.

I am supported by other life forms like trees, birds, insects, animals, and plants... as are we all. We do nothing on our own. I hear the music of the flute... the sound that is carried in the whispers of the wind.

Tree stump, UBC, Vancouver, BC, Canada 2018

TREE: *I am an old one who lived for close to 200 years. I was the grandmother cedar for this area near Wreck Beach.*

Through my roots, I sent messages to the whole forest. When the little trees around me became big enough, I sent out my life energy to support them.

I called in the lightning to help my transition from grandmother tree to nurse tree. One bold strike of lightning to my trunk and the first little tree was energised to help grow companion plant medicines all around its base. These plants support the community of new life among the trees.

Now, the little sapling trees grow from my experience. And the tree network under the ground supports my presence in the form of a stump.

Tree in Nitobe Gardens, UBC, Vancouver, BC, Canada 2018

TREE: *I was planted to honour the Japanese tradition of bonsai. As a mountain juniper, I grow and twist as an illusion to dance in the wind. But these twists and turns take many years to develop as they do in life. It is not an instant happening.*

My presence at UBC Nitobe gardens is a reminder of the strength and stamina required to face life each day. This is also the way of students who travel here from many different countries.

The road may be hard and, at times, disappear. But one footstep after another, you can find what is needed to go your own way. All those who went before you will help. You need no eyes to feel their presence guiding you in the right direction. Have faith and hold the course.

Ask the hardest questions of yourself. Be attentive and have faith. Your cry for help is always heard by the trees around you.

Tree on Cortes Island, BC, Canada 2018

TREE: *I am the one who bridges earth and sky. I am very old in your time. But this is not the same timeline as mine. I was here before civilization existed as you know it.*

Near the creek, I witnessed many humans and their love and respect for water to bathe, drink, and for spiritual cleansing. They spoke to me as I now speak to you. Then came others who seemed to be in a big hurry. But for those who take time to listen, I am still here.

I am home to infinite civilizations of winged ones, insects, moss, plants, lichen. This cosmos is tapped deep within the soil, where fungus, worms, and roots dive into the earth and pull the inner earth realms up into the sweet sap, nourishing the branches and my greenery high above.

My message to you is to sit or stand peacefully in the forest and listen to your breath. The inflow and the outflow... your ancestors are with you in each moment, as am I. My thick bark protects me and connects me to earth and sky. You stand before me in the middle... both feet on the ground, and I can feel your presence in my smallest roots deep down in the earth. The forest all around is aware of your presence and there is constant communication.

Hear that creek? I am also in that creek, pulling precious droplets of water up into the very top of my crown.

Do you hear the birds? My boughs offer safety and protection for the nestlings.

Do you see the smaller trees all around me? We are intertwined in a community of information and share our energy.

The Tree Whisperer

You may think I am dead... but there is still juice in my core. See all the little saplings I am supporting that grow on my branches? They carry all the wisdom from my roots.

I invite you to take your shoes off and walk barefoot in this forest and our knowledge will become a part of you. Much gratitude for your presence on this path.

2019

Tree in central square, Puerto Vallarta, Mexico, 2019

TREE: *Hola. My name is Guardian of the Square. I have seen many changes in this city. (Tree on left of photo.)*

My message is that no matter where humans travel, they are connected to the earth, and the more they travel, the more they create positive energy fields between locations. Imagine how birds travel between trees carrying seeds... this diversity brings strength into the community. We work together as a connected group of living beings.

A forest was here long ago, but now, a community square. We trees have an opportunity here to really grow and occupy the space. Here, there are lots of interactions between people, animals, and nature. These spaces are invaluable to humans as they restore their connection to the earth and offer regenerative input. For us trees, we are the chosen few to take on the role of inter-species communicators. The largest of us holds the energy for the entire community of trees. That's me!

In this square, we have seen the change from a small fishing village to a huge international city with people from all over the world. The location is unique now as it is filled with diverse cultures, wanderers, and locals creating a hum and bustle of activity. The simple fishing village morphs as the cosmopolitan city weaves the fabric of a bustling community.

We trees are rooted to one location here, and yet, through thoughts and feelings from all over the planet, a new template is being created. We trees are like the antennas for the energetic communication that goes on between people and nature. My trunk is strong and my root system vast. This allows me to guard the interactions of the entire square and all who come here.

In the past, the people were simpler and more direct. Everyone lived very close to nature. Now, technology has changed your relationship to the natural world. In the future, the presence of the trees will become top priority for humanity to work to heal the planet from the effects of industrial pollution. Although technology connects the minds of humans, you still require the physical presence of trees for your heart connection to the earth.

This square is constantly in transition just like the passersby. The markets here attract ideas and people from all over the world. When they walk on this ground, they are energised by being in the presence of trees. This, in turn, becomes integrated into their being and, when they leave to go home, they are different than when they first came. Spending time with me is like a complete battery recharge for humans.

Each human also carries energy from their unique political, social, and economic circumstances. We obtain information from them and change and shift. It is a mutually beneficial exchange. We trees are aware of the vibrational fields of information. In my experience, not all humans identify with this common knowledge. Back in the old times, many people understood this connection... that has changed as your idea of time has sped up. We have compassion for you humans struggling to understand the invisible world that is supporting all.

Michelle Beauregard

My message is for humans to take some time to walk amongst the trees and feel the intuitive connection that is beyond words.

Thank you for taking the time to connect and put the message out about us trees and nature. Much gratitude.

Tree in market, Puerto Vallarta, Mexico, 2019

TREE: *Much gratitude for sitting here in my presence. I am known as the guide. My roots tell the story. The river here is my connecting force to all humans. They come here to get drinking water and trade goods. I have many roots that cover the earth and tap into the water source underneath your feet.*

The water source is also a source of life energy.

Taking many forms, I absorb infinite grace in my being. Taking water, I transfer the rushing flow into my core.

The water criss-crosses my branches like many hands collecting rain.

The elementals dwell within my core... their ancient senses are at one with my consciousness. They can be seen from your inner vision.

Humans may experience this powerful life presence through the many animal forms that inhabit my tranquil space and take the shape of birds, iguanas, snakes, or bugs.

Messengers that inhabit a dream world... they are a part of the play of energy... shifting their awareness in and out of your time. Some beings have been with me since the beginning of time. Their songs are now mine.

Place your ears on my trunk and listen within. Their stirrings and movements will take you into the past, deep in the earth beyond this day and into realms of magic and medicine of the plants.

I have witnessed the coming and going of many people whose lives depended on the fresh water. Their laughter, tears and bones buried deep under my massive root system. Some came with honest intention and others with murderous eyes.

The lost ones creep around me at night... they are the souls of many men who lost their way. They are wanderers or hungry ghosts who search for humans, who are out of their body (due to intoxication) and can now provide a living body for the lost ones to experience the human activities they are still craving. That is why people do things they would not usually do while intoxicated. While you humans are not in your bodies, then you are open to anything.

In the light of the day, these lost ones must go back into the cracks of darkness.

I reach out to humans who come here to rejuvenate and be in nature. You can see how my branches look like benches for people to sit under.

Many years ago, people would come to me to make deals for barter and trade. Some deals were done with those from faraway lands. The treachery of greed caught on like wildfire... some lost everything, including their lives. Others took advantage of the moment and got rich from the earth. The price that we trees paid was high as many of us lost our lives in the humans' quest for more and more. We were cut down and cleared with no thought of the value of living ecosystems.

This is my legacy... and now it is yours to share.

Tree in Sayulita Square, Mexico, 2019

TREE: *I am the sacred mother tree of the centre plaza.*

All of life is sacred and I hold the space where people come to remember this. Here, the Indigenous people sell their art. They have been coming to this location for many years. They bring the energy of the mountains in their vibration and by connecting with people from around the world, their vision of peace and harmony is spread into the fifth dimension to travel into the planetary consciousness.

I transmute this message into my roots, up my trunk, out of my branches, and into my leaves. I have three trunks to represent divinity.

During the day, I release this cosmic connectivity to all who assemble in this square. Special ceremonies are conducted under my branches to mark the lunar calendar and seasonal celebrations.

We are all related... as a mother tree, I support all those who have passed and provide information to those who are here.

I am here to remind YOU of your sacred nature. Take this message to humanity:

There is never-ending energy for the highest good available, even during the darkest days and, if you hold the belief in your heart, the trees will support every step of your life, even long after your physical body has returned to the earth. This is my divine appointment in Sayulita, the magical town.

Tree on road, Puerto Vallarta, Mexico 2019

TREE: *I appear to be by myself, but I am strongly connected to all that goes on here. My roots are the strength of the structure of all human activity... the traffic and pedestrian movement energises me. The more the structure needs support, the more roots I send down into the ground.*

In this community, everybody is overworked... they carry heavy loads... too much to sustain. Whether their burden is physical or emotional, eventually... they get tired out, but I am here to remind them that they are not by themselves. For every bit they carry, I reach out to help balance the load, too. My gnarled roots remind them that time passes. Our strength may weaken as we grow older but our connection to the land and community keeps us going. Although our support may seem to crumble at times around us, our entire environment is supportive of our day-to-day existence. The road I am growing out of seems to be in great disrepair... I find ways to adapt and gather the strength to carry on. This life force is all around each of us.

Gratitude is the key.

Tree on trail, Yelapa, Mexico 2019

TREE: *My name is Embrace. I send out energy by holding onto all that is around me. My branches intertwine with the earth, rocks, and concrete. My strength comes from merging with things that you humans might see as obstacles or difficulties to my growth. These so-called challenges, in fact, help me to gain strength and adaptability.*

But this story is one that has more beneath the surface than you can imagine. What you might perceive as an impossible place to grow is, for me, a place filled with my two most important conditions to grow... love and light.

I have been here for over 70 years. When I first started growing, this place was truly wild and not populated by many humans. There was a footpath along the sea, but it had dense jungle along one side. Fishermen used to come by and launch their boats off the rocks.

One fisherman decided to move his family out here. He worked to clear the trail and put some rocks to stabilise the sandy soil. It was rough but passable for his family. Every day, he would move a few heavy stones until, eventually, there was a little area for him to sit and enjoy the view. He would come here every day and watch the sunset. When he finally became old and passed away, his family sprinkled his ashes under me... among the rocks he had so carefully carried and placed at my base.

As I grew over the years, my roots reached around all the stones and held onto them like precious jewels in his memory. All his love and devotion to this location was like nourishment for my branches.

MICHELLE BEAUREGARD

I guess you could say this is a communication of the love that lives among my roots; the fisherman's essence of joy for this place is made available for all who pass under my branches.

Tree on street of Romantic Zone, Puerto Vallarta, Mexico 2019

TREE: *I have lived here for the past 60 years. My message for the people of this community is to reach out to each other as I am doing in my place. I sit on one side of the street, but I cross to the other side and between houses to connect the whole area. By growing roots in the community, I stay strong. A variety of locations and homes and families gives me diversity in terms of energy. I transmute the energy from the earth into the air, bringing fresh perspective in my leaves and branches.*

My structure covers the neighbourhood like a hat... all different parts of the same location feeding energetically from the roots of the earth where people conduct their daily business. I provide shade and a cool space for humans and animal life. I move in the wind and bring new thoughts and emotions to all who are around in a grounded way. I lean over the street to connect those who are lonely and need support with others, reaching out always... my bark is tough to withstand the bumps of daily life. Humans also need thick skin to withstand the knocks of life.

My seed pods are a reminder that death and life are all wrapped up together. What looks discarded is the seed for a new life in nature's cycle. Humans must remember this too. We are all part of the same cycle. We tap into each other's energy fields and spread our thoughts throughout our homes and towns, and this leaves an imprint. Each of us is like the branch of a tree... we feed, support, and nourish our environment in so many ways.

My message for the humans is to be aware of the community of nature in your home territory and look after and nourish it as it sustains you and your family's good life. We must work together to keep it all together. Gracias.

Tree in romantic zone, Puerto Vallarta, Mexico 2019

TREE: *My age is unknown... I have been here since long before the streets existed with only footpaths. I grow along the trail of the people of the land. Farmers, carrying their earth-warmed fruit and vegetables to market. They travel a long way to make the most of the busy markets. Many come to trade for fish from the sea. Back and forth and back and forth... always movement beneath my branches and into my roots. The cobblestone streets were laid stone by stone to commemorate a successful city and its people. The land is rich... the people take what they need to survive and thrive in the abundance. My roots curl and twist over the sidewalks reaching out to connect to this still ever-changing movement of people.*

First, they travelled barefoot, walking contentedly among the forest trees, sounds of talking and laughter captured in my leaves and rustled into my branches.

Over 100 years ago, an old man died while sleeping against my trunk—his body small and fragile. I held him for a while until his soul passed through the core of my being.

I reach out and help those who need it, my presence a calming balm for the heart and spirit. When he was younger, that same old man, then a small boy, sat with his back against my trunk, much as you are now: taking a few moments to eat lunch after a busy day at the market, breathing in the quiet strength of my branches. I came to know his skipping footsteps as he travelled past once a week from his family home with fruit to sell.

As he grew into a young man, I enjoyed hearing his conversation with the girl he loved as they sat and picnicked in the shade.

Years later, with a family of his own, I experienced, through his heart, the great love he had for his children as they all came together for the big market day. The joy of their laughter and play filled me with much contentment. As the man grew older, he slowed, and his grandchildren held his wrinkled hands and playfully poked his stomach as they stopped to enjoy a bite to eat. His wife just stopped accompanying him one day... and I felt his loss as though one of my roots had been cut off. His quiet tears dropped onto the earth, and I caught them, sending the sadness up and out into the sunshine on my leaves.

His daughter walked with him after that... or he would shuffle along slowly by himself, his back bent and crooked like my trunk. His last day on this earth, he came to me like an old friend and sat in his usual way with his back resting against me, feet outstretched. I felt his last breath escape and sit like a butterfly in the dappled light of my leaves. A smile on his sun-weathered face and his hands lying peacefully on his chest. His life's story is now part of mine as we are entwined together in time and space.

He lived in gratitude, and I felt his connection to all the earth. No separation between us, his heartbeat now a quiet whisper in my boughs. If you close your eyes and listen deeply, you can hear it.

2020

Tree in London, UK 2020

TREE: *My name is Chester the Third. I am 500 years old. The roots of my lineage trace back to the time the original church was here. I was planted after a fire from a previous tree that grew in this area.*

This church sits on sacred soil and has for many centuries. Before organised religions, this earth was the site of pantheistic rituals and ceremonies in keeping with the natural world. In fact, the bones of a dragon that used to protect this sacred area lie under the church. The dragon was not from this place but came from afar. The energy of this creature remains.

The collective memories of these places can touch the hearts of those in this present day and those from the past. It is a deep feeling of connection to those who walked the earth before.

I sit here reminding people that their roots run deep and that there are a great number of mysteries yet to be explored. Know what gives you strength and joy... tap into that sweetness. Chestnuts represent abundance for humanity. It takes humility to see how the chestnut harvest is very precious and must not be wasted.

Tree grove near grave of Karl Marx, London, UK 2020

TREE GROVE: *Wise are the words of those who lie buried deep in the earth. You walk upon their bones. The soles of your feet pulling at the souls of those ancestors who are restless with yearning. For although they lie in a terminal state, there exists a part of them within the collective of humanity. Their stories are merely under the surface, and when you come to honour those who walked the earth short years ago, they come to life.*

Let the written word direct your world... and you will meet an uncertain fate, for our intellect—the intellect of one—is not enough. Better to rule one's own destiny by the heart and step out of rules. Work with lightness in your heart and let light be your guide.

The systems that rule your world now are headed for collapse... that is the destiny of all systems. Out of chaos will come a more humane and just world.

Yours is a time that I do not understand... a collapse of all systems that requires a dimension beyond philosophy. I am excited for a new era where people wake up. Most are in a deep slumber.

Protect your ideals inside your heart... a new time is coming.

My philosophical thoughts for the new manuscript in politics are still evolving... I pick up on these thought forms.

I am a tree with memories in the ground and they are constantly in circulation. The new philosophy is all about connecting to the natural world. Listen deeply. My silence is golden.

Tree on canal, London, UK 2020

TREE: *Water Walker is the name you can call me. I come from a family of water walkers. Our roots tap into the canal and feed from the energy of all those living on or near the water.*

The canal brings new energy deep into the heart of the city. The flow of water cleanses and restores stagnant areas. We water walkers share the transformation of this stagnant water by drawing water into our limbs and releasing it.

Canal culture is old and involves bringing new ideas in the form of goods and people. Trade and barter have always been a part of London. Physically, the canal's historical purpose has changed, more for recreation now. But the water flow remains a kind of carrier for traditions and a way of life that is close to being forgotten.

Without the canals, we trees would not be here... as we are drawing from the energy lines in the water.

The water is no longer clean... but we trees can filter it into use for our needs. Humans have always lived close to water and these canals remind us of the old ways.

The world is changing fast, and we are rooted in the past. But water will always find a way and its levels move dramatically over the centuries. We feel that, in the future, the water levels will keep rising... then we will become another part of the collective memory. The water walker trees of the canal will carry a story beyond our own existence by communicating to layers deep within the earth.

Tree on Hampstead Heath, London, UK 2020

TREE: *My age... it is not appropriate to tell a lady's age, but never mind...*

I am 500 years old. My name is M'lady.

My presence is but a small part of the entire group of trees here in Hampstead Heath. In the 1300s, this was a wilderness place where people came to rest, often overnight on their way to the London Town.

At my roots, people have died and even given birth while on the road south. One woman and her newborn are buried here beneath my roots. They came in search of the baby's father, who had never returned from his journey to visit relatives.

I embrace them in my growth and their essence runs in my limbs.

I am not the first tree to grow here... I rise above an older mother tree. We are a tree family much like a human family... we have multiple generations, we come from seed, we grow and eventually become new fertile ground for the next generations.

The young woman and her child buried with us are a beautiful metaphor for the family tree.

We are always thinking of the coming generations, sharing resources with them to promote growth of the forest or community of which we are a part.

On my trunk, you can see fungus and moss—other living organisms that contribute to our lifecycle. In decay is growth and, in growth, the rhythms of the seasons.

The benefits of sitting under my branches are multidimensional... I will lift your heart and synchronise it to the heart of the forest. You will leave here feeling grounded and connected in ways you did not before you came. The heartbeat of the forest runs under the earth and is not audible with the ear. But if you place your hands anywhere on my trunk, the synchronisation will occur of its own accord.

You have travelled far... I am a resting place for travellers... put your feet on the bare earth and be welcomed by nature.

Tree at Westminster Abbey, London, UK 2020

TREE: *I am called Christopher. After the saint.*

Come under my protection and be saved from your worldly cares. The guide and protector of the gates to the realm of divine appointment. All the riches of the land are not in a single silver coin nor the amassing of great wealth through title, rank, and seal. The real wealth comes from gratitude to those that went before us... our footsteps are in pace with the ghosts of the past.

The treasure is abundance in your blood lineage so that you can ask for assistance from them at any time. I am one of those keepers of the past, memories held in my roots, released by acknowledging our connection to all that is and all that was.

Those who come here to worship are seeking connection. May you find peace in nature and purify your heart by good deeds.

In my time, I have felt the pounding of bombs all around me, people running in fear, and people seeking refuge. These are themes that repeat... in history and in the present day.

Humans can shift this war-like state... it takes just one person to start. Any one of you can be that person. All of nature supports you. Take heed that you are of immense value.

Tree in London, UK 2020

TREE: *You come at an interesting time. My name is Godspeed.*

This area was a munitions transfer point to get to ships for the king's military. There was a busy dock with many people loading and unloading artillery and supplies.

In the spot where I am, many people were heading off to bigger ships along the coast. This was a location for goodbyes and fine farewells. Many a young man bid farewell to life as a Londoner as he set sail for faraway places and battles unknown.

Other times, prisoners were shipped from this area to Westminster Court and ferried back again to meet their fate. Some prisoners managed to escape with the help of smugglers. Many were wished "Godspeed" for their journey. Many prisoners were beheaded or left to languish within the prison walls behind me.

This area was a "meeting" point for many people in London at that time. So, the memory in my roots is mostly of the comings and goings along the Thames River.

At this point in time, I am a witness to many people from all countries travelling through to learn about London's history. I hear languages that come from all points on the planet.

The wars of the old days no longer exist in a physical way. But their collective memory still lingers within each person... no matter where they originate. This is a perfect time to reflect on the future as living beings who are a part of the circle of life. Learn and remember who you are... then take the next steps *with great love. We are here for such a short while... but the more humans connect with the mass consciousness of trees, the more energy we will have to evolve in a positive direction.*

Tree at Notre Dame Church, Paris, France 2020

TREE: *I am our lady's court—Lady of the Court. My wisdom lies in the ages of the earth I grow in... 400 years in the making. Notre Dame is the name you humans refer to this place as. I know it as the sacred court.*

The church bells ring for those who wait. The soulful confessions of bygone eras lie deep within the soil. I hold a memory of all those asking here for forgiveness—thief or king.

My branches reach out beyond these sacred grounds... over the sharp metal points of the fence to help heal the wounds of any past injustices for all those who walk by.

At one point, the gardeners cut off a sharp piece of fence that kept cutting into my limb and injuring it again and again. They realised that I was more important than the fence they were trying to preserve. The scars on my branch are there to this day—a reminder that the will to live is strong and that I have rights as any other living being.

Still, my branches are cut if they are seen to be a hazard, but I just keep reaching out towards the people to remind them to have hope and that we are connected.

Tree in Montmartre, Paris, France 2020

TREE: *Bonjour! My name is Gigi.*

The artists gather here each day, their brush strokes finding a way to etch the colour and life of Paris. Some are here for inspiration and others for survival. It has always been so.

The collective memory of this place is rich in culture and colour. The remembrances of those who came before now linger in the movement of my leaves. The shadows of artists long since passed flicker among the cobblestones.

We trees absorb the thoughts and whispering of those who have gathered here for hundreds of years. Their song becomes our song as we watch the seasons pass in a never-ending symphony of sound, light, and colour.

Yellow urges us to reach for the sky in the form of spring sunshine.

Green covers us in a coat of shining radiant foliage.

Red encircles our roots and sends signals for us to keep connected to the community. Bright flowers, cafes, and fashion.

Blue radiates from the azure sky, connecting trees and people under one giant umbrella of sight and sound.

All these colours filter through our branches and send us signals from the palette of nature. The living art of being here in a moment of joy. So many moments strung together in timeless days.

Tree in Citadel Park, Paris, France 2020

The Tree Whisperer

TREE: *Trees in this park were sewn with the intention of benefitting the next generations... the French aesthetic of landscaping and gardens is also an imprint going back hundreds of years. All the thousands of hours that gardeners put into making this beautiful place of natural refuge still resonate today with all who come from around the world.*

Around us, we have the sun on the grass and the gentle breeze blowing, creating a refuge for all beings. So, although we are part of a man-made environment, our presence is a reminder to coexist with nature whenever possible.

Take time to sit outside in the sun amongst us... feel the warmth penetrate your bones and know it is good.

Tree in Trocadero, Paris, France 2020

TREE: *Paris... filled with creative ideas and joie de vivre— one of the highest vibration cities due to the artists gathering here from all over the world.*

The generations of creativity create a collective memory that ignites ideas and inspiration in all who come here.

There was no mistake that the Tour de Eiffel was built here as this is now a place that lifts the spirit and dreams of the next generatio

Tree in Fromentine, Isle-de-Yeu, France 2020

TREE: *The incessant wind bends and shapes my branches. The winter storms here are so intense that the people come and cut my branches, so they don't break and fall on passersby.*

The people, like the tree, are hardy and adaptable, fitting their environment with great strength.

If there is friction between people, they can just escape to the outdoors and breathe in the salty air.

We beach trees enjoy our lonely, windswept landscape this time of year for, in the summer, there are thousands of humans everywhere.

In times past, fishermen cast their nets and ventured out into the wild Atlantic Sea, never knowing when, or if, they would return but feeling the call of their longing flowing through their bones... binding them to an unspoken contract between nature and man... the tides of time are all they could agree upon.

Many fishermen and their families from long ago brought special talismans from their homes and sometimes tossed them into the sea as an offering for safe passage. Many of those talismans are buried in the sand near my roots. The hopes and wishes of those who never returned now joins the sorrow of those left behind. Their lament is heard in whispers along this seashore at night. Today, the tiny feet of laughing children playing on the beach, echoes to be heard like waves lapping on the sand.

Tree on Isle-de-Yeu, France, 2020

TREE: *The wind carried you here to this place of learning. The winds of many countries and faraway places pass over my branches. In the air, the thoughts of many people are carried through time and space. The four wind directions are powerful. This is an island of seafaring people and the old ways of navigating the seas involved naming the winds after the four cardinal points we now call north, south, east, and west.*

The East wind is the energy of youth and creativity... this wind is a friend of mine.

The North wind comes from the realm of the elders... the wise ones are among us always. The biting cold makes us trees strong and resilient like the people of this island.

The South wind is the powerful force of Africa and the Atlantic... There comes with this wind many new ideas and changes. Sometimes, this change is dramatic, and one will never be the same after riding the waves of life into the future using only trust to navigate from places unknown.

The wind from the West is an invitation to learn new things... gentle rolling waves, this is the age of maturity and growth. I use this wind to dance with joy.

If my branches break with the wind, it is my unwillingness to bend and move with the rhythms of the air.

Rooted into the sea, I carry the memories of many ships coming and going.

This island beckons people and their dreams. I feel the memory of those who came before me long ago in this harbour. Some came looking for a simpler life connected to the sea. Once here, they became solid like the rocks of the shoreline. Their energy runs deep like my roots.

The winds and sands of time shift so that all can view their lives like the rising and setting of the sun. A moment of light playing on the oceans of time.

Tree in Chambolle-Musigny, France 2020

TREE: *I am the tree of this village holding the energy for the people in this community. Solid... adaptable... connected to the earth. This once was a place where the women of the village came to do ceremonies for the earth. A healing spring bubbled, and many came to be healed.*

In this place where I grow, women would meet from around the countryside, bringing their herbs, potions, and healing salves.

An old woman who was the town's herbalist in the 1800s had her ashes placed at the bottom of my roots when she passed away. Her knowledge and information can be accessed by tapping into my roots.

For example, for gout, yellow flowers are a remedy. I am a Linden tree.

My specialty is to provide information about nature's medicine.

That is why I have been here for so long... providing information to those who need it.

Plant knowledge sometimes appears to come from the people, but we are all part of a network of plants and healers working together. It has been this way for many generations. Those seeking knowledge of the healing properties of the land will be able to access this botanical information when they are ready—if they are open to receive.

Thank you for taking the time to honour the ones who went before... their knowledge will never disappear. It is imprinted in our local forest community.

Tree in Black Lake, Switzerland 2020

TREE (the tree I am standing beside): *I am the guardian of this land and house for the past 100 years. The woman who lives here in this house is the head of the family, just as I am the head of the forest in this place. We look out for each other.*

The small ones live in another dimension but are very close to me. Little gnome families used to be near the creek all the time. Now, they are not so present in this dimension as people have forgotten their existence.

Wee tiny beings are from nature and live closely to nature... but they are in a place invisible to the eye.

The Solomon clan of gnomes live on this land. It's a good home with a little creek and many berries in the summer. They are the messengers between nature and human families. They encourage gardens, animals, and bird life.

I talk to you about the unseen dimension because you have taken the time to access my knowledge, and so your interest brings up my secrets. Known to many in this area... not forgotten... but only in the flicker of shadows do you feel the presence of the little people.

I am a part of this special place in the world where the little people bring old traditions to the surface. Listen to the wind, the thunder, the water... they all speak to you in some old familiar language beyond words and beyond time.

Tree in Zurich, Switzerland, 2020

TREE: *My name is Aunty. My home is here, with the children. I have been here since the 1930s.*

I was planted here by an old woman who always helped look after many children when she was young. She was self-sufficient and strong, with a big heart to match. She lived right in this neighbourhood and came from the mountains. She missed the children of her mountain home but abided here because of her husband's family and his work. Every day, she came to meet with other families and watch the children play. In her later years, she would just sit quietly and the joy she felt fills this space with much love.

The fun, light energy of her intention to create a space for children has remained.

This little area was empty for many years during the war. Only the children remained, either at school or in the apartments. That was a time of great fear. Such is the state of the world during war. Some men of the village would gather here for quiet discussions about local politics and town gossip.

After the war, there was a release of tension as people reoriented their lives. The children have returned and now a playground is at my roots.

The love from the woman who planted me endures and I continue to share this energy with all the children and parents who visit in the park.

Tree at La Sagrada Familia, Barcelona, Spain 2020

TREE: *My name is Grace. Thank you for stopping to make contact. It is by nature's grace that you stand here next to me. All the elements in the natural world since the beginning of time have brought you and I together at this moment.*

My message for you is that all people are part of our sacred family.

My branches reach towards La Sagrada Familia... an architectural beacon of devotion and dedication to all of life. Each one of us has life energy and this force is present in all things.

My branches are reaching towards the Sagrada. I am a part of this environment. It is my nature to celebrate the reflection of the divine love of artist Antoni Gaudi's masterpiece made with his devotion to a higher purpose. People from all over the world come here to witness this expression of creativity and divine glory.

This park is a mirror image of the Sagrada... the Sagrada was created with special attention given to the aesthetic of trees, grass, birds, greenery, and flowers in the design and architecture.

The vibration of all these people coming to visit this place is truly radiant and feeds the soul like a magnetic force attracting positive feelings of light and beauty. I am a part of this forcefield, and my branches can't help but reach towards the front doors of the cathedral.

I was planted at the same time as work on this cathedral started. Now, I continue to grow and support the foundations of Gaudi's work.

Tree in Park Guell, Barcelona, Spain 2020

TREE: *I am called Mirador. Roots reaching like ancient fingers caressing the stones, dirt, and mountains. I carry the memories from hundreds of years of humanity. My sense of time crawls through the sediment of human experience.*

On these mountain tops floats higher vibrational energy than below. This is a place of meditation, reflection, and rejuvenation. Below us, the lower realms of physical day-to-day life take hold.

Gaudi's art also raises the vibration of any location. His intention to create with a dedication to God, in the form of nature, connects us to his work. That is why so many people come here. Attracted to the good feelings of nature and the clear headspace above the everyday mundane.

My presence is to share this food for the soul by stretching across and above the earth and into the sky.

Lift your eyes and feel the medicine of presence, of being in the moment. All around you are grow plant medicines that are pure and powerful. The olive trees below you are very old and have a connection to these mountains, as do I.

We are a network of living beings in the community. For although we have no eyes, we see all.

Although we have no ears, we hear all.

Although we have no mouths, we speak the truth. Although we have no hands, we touch your heart.

My message to the people of Barcelona is to go to the nature places in your city and you will be healed from the stresses of life. Seek these places often... we always respond to your needs. Giving gratitude to Gaudi for his art reflects the beauty of a flower, the simplicity of a leaf and radiance of a tree. His work is a healing legacy for all humanity.

Tree in Barcelona, Spain, 2020

TREE: *My bark is old and twisted ... a reflection of the twists and turns in society.*

Barcelona is a city that is independent, proud, and fierce.

The changes in the state of politics affect me little... for the blood of the people runs through the streets and into my roots.

We are survivors and will continue to thrive just as the mountains of the north guard our solidarity to this land and its people.

See my branches... lush and green... fed by countless underground streams of water that hold the energy of many thousands of warriors.

Tree in Cascada del Parc de la Ciutadella, Barcelona, Spain 2020

TREE: *What do you see in the pond that sits beneath me?*

Drink from my roots... it's a place of great serenity.

The water reflects the sky and acts as a mirror for light and sunshine.

What do you see in the pond?

Green is the colour of my leaves. The heart of a tree can be found in a single leaf. Each leaf, a tiny form of the larger.

At this waterfall, we create a refuge for birds, humans, and many infinite life forms.

My roots go deep under the pond.

I am larger under the water than I am above it. Not all is as it seems. Roots travelling under the water and earth sending information out in all directions through water, soil, and sky.

Just like you humans... we are each smaller versions of the bigger picture called Earth. Your signals start as thoughts and then become activity. Know that your signals are heard. May they resonate in beauty.

Tree in Parc de la Ciutadella, Barcelona, Spain, 2020

TREE: *The music of life is all around you. I am called the symphony of green life. Sinfonía de la Vida Verde.*

The parakeets' bright green feathers resonate with us trees, their calls a connection to higher realms of consciousness.

In troubled times, these reminders are so invaluable as they raise the field of awareness.

Each of us trees in this park are antennae for the bird life—transmitting the joy and energy of song, and the wonder of life.

The birds, in turn, enjoy our branches as nesting spots and places of refuge.

We all work together to create a paradise on earth and as a reminder that all of life is sacred. Gratitude for you taking the time to tap into the music of life!

*Stockholm Library,
Stockholm, 2020*

TREE: *Hello!*

The library draws those wishing to immerse themselves in the realm of the intellect: a space where ideas flow and bring together new inspiration, new thoughts.

The root of all learning is the desire for knowledge. Many have entered the library every day now for over 100 years... searching for an immersion into the shelves of books.

The buzz of the mind creates thought forms, and these thought forms create energy. Following energy, there comes action.

The mind can create a haven or an escape from the daily routine.

Libraries are the essence of our cultural, political, and geographic history.

What about the unspoken stories from those who are forgotten from the pages of the books...?

My branches pick up all the thoughts of those who come here. Each person is a living, breathing storybook—a page-less being immersed in the day-to-day business of life.

There are no lesser or greater minds, for the source of thoughts comes from the infinite possibilities of time and space. I absorb the intentions of those coming here with a purpose.

Deep below this building, my roots trace an ancient legacy of this city. The ideas of those with whom I connect flow through the vast network of roots, dirt, water, and stone. Recycling the past and re-writing the moments... with each generation, the cycles of learning repeat. Each one of us is a unique chapter in the book of existence.

Who are you?

We are so much larger than we think. A massive neural network stretching above and below the ground. I am a physical manifestation of all those who thought me into this reality. We are in this together.

Take a moment to reach into the knowledge of your family history and, like a vast library, you can locate the volumes of information.

Their story is a part of you.

2022

Apple Tree, Kaslo BC 2022

It seems fitting that the last story in the book comes from my mother-in-law, Wanja's apple tree in her front yard. This was her home for 40 years and the first Reiki center in Canada created in 1980. I have been living here for the past two years after she passed away and this is where much of this book was written.

TREE: The apple does not fall far from the tree. My roots determine my health on all levels, intellectually, emotionally, physically, and spiritually.

The harvest of apples is a gift from the seed I came from many years ago. In each seed there exists a forest. The forest represented in every seed carries all the wisdom of the lineage I came from. In the cold times, we trees are dormant, and all the energy is placed into the roots under the surface of the earth. In the spring, we blossom with beauty, colour, and fragrance.

I do not experience emotion as humans but do have a sense of connection to our community. When it is in balance and harmony, so am I.

My physical health is determined by my family tree and the physical surroundings, including all life forms as well as rocks, mountains, water, air, and earth.

The spiritual aspect of my existence is created by my interconnectedness to the other plant, animal, and human forms around us. My daily interactions are recorded within my energy field, and I can share this energy with others. I am also able to cleanse and take away negative emotions from humans. Humans and other life forms may also give me beneficial or healing energy. The stars, planets, sun, and moon radiate their energy affecting the growth pattern of us trees, and this includes bestowing us with healing gifts.

I am on a star path that allows energy to transmit from the stars to this location. This constellation trail is very powerful with a variety of different contact points along Kootenay Lake.

Trees operate on a different timeline, so I can contact past, present, and future. This gives me the unique ability to share stories of long ago.

The apple of knowledge from me can be held in one's hand, and when you take a bite there is a sweet taste that awaits.

Some people can digest only a little knowledge from this apple, so the rest waits. Others may find one apple only awakens a taste for more.

An entire bushel of apples may fill up the root cellar but must wait until the right season to be processed.

The seeds of knowledge always ripen at the right moment. All four seasons are of value. At times, wisdom and knowledge elude us but patience bears fruit in time.

I have experienced many seasons and watched the children of your family and others play as children and then become adults with children of their own.

The warm winds of summer blow through my branches, bringing the ripest apples falling to the ground where new seeds are sewn. It takes time for roots to grow but when they take hold in the earth, a mighty tree sprouts filled with promise and sweet possibilities for growth and harvest.

A Call to Action

It is my hope that this book will encourage others to go outdoors and take the time to connect to the trees. This collection of stories is offered as a gift that can take Reiki practitioners to deeper levels of awareness in their daily practice.

There is no proper technique required, just an open mind and trusting in what information comes up.

The trees are always in our presence and their voices can be heard in the peacefulness of inner silence.

The best way to immerse into the world of trees is to take the first step and let your intuition guide you.

We plan to continue our tree whispering travels and writings, so if you have some trees you would like to connect with near you and are interested in a workshop or virtual tutorial on tree communications, please send us an email to see what is possible.

If you are interested in purchasing any of Wanja Twan's Reiki books, we are the distributors. You can find out more about her books on our "Reiki books by Wanja Twan"

Facebook page.
EMAIL contact: distantstar100@gmail.com

Author's Biography

In 1993, I left a career as a documentary journalist in Toronto, Ontario to return home to Vancouver, British Columbia. While there, I met my future husband. Shortly after, we moved to an off-grid homestead in the coastal mountains. Without electricity or a phone, my sensitivity to the energy in the forest around me grew, sparking an immense sense of wonder in the natural world that I had missed while living in Toronto. The trees played their part in calling me home to speak.

During the next five years living off-the-grid, the trees, plants, birds, and animals became a part of my day-to-day life. I saw in a new way that our human-made world, the creations of science and technology, can be out of harmony with nature. I became aware that being in nature helped me live a life more in balance and more in tune with my environment through a web of invisible networks.

Using my Reiki practise as a foundation for connecting with trees, I realised quite unexpectedly that there were mysteries to be discovered in the form of remarkable stories from the trees.

www.ingramcontent.com/pod-product-compliance
Lightning Source LLC
Chambersburg PA
CBHW042329150426
43193CB00005B/55